Welcome

I am so glad you are here! Before we begin this new session, I want to take the time and let you know that YOU have been prayed for! It is not a coincidence you are participating in this online Bible study.

My prayer for you this session is simple: **that you will grow closer to our Lord as you dig into His Word each and every day!** As you develop the discipline of being in God's Word on a daily basis, I pray you will fall in love with Him even more as you spend time reading from the Bible.

Each day before you read the assigned Scripture(s), pray and ask God to help you understand it. Invite Him to speak to you through His Word. Then listen. **It's His job to speak to you and your job to listen and obey.**

Take time to read the verses over and over again. We are told in Proverbs to *search and you will find.*

> *"Search for it like silver, and hunt for it like hidden treasure. Then you will understand."*

We are thrilled to provide many different resources for you as you participate in our online Bible study:
- Growing Through Prayer Study Journal (print out or purchase online)
- Reading Plan
- Weekly Blog posts (Mondays, Wednesdays, & Fridays)
- Weekly Memory Verses
- Weekly Monday Videos
- Weekly Challenges
- Online community: Facebook, Twitter, Instagram, LoveGodGreatly.com
- Hashtags: #LoveGodGreatly #GrowingThroughPrayer

All of us here at Love God Greatly can't wait to get started with you and hope to see you at the finish line. **Endure, persevere, press on – and don't give up!** Let's finish well what we are beginning today. We will be here every step of the way, *cheering you on!* **We are in this together.** Fight to rise early, to push back the stress of the day, to sit alone and spend time in God's Word! I can't wait to see what God has in store for us this session!

Journey with us as we learn to **Love God Greatly** with our lives!!!

Table of Contents

Our Community

Love God Greatly consists of a beautiful community of women who use a variety of technology platforms to keep each other accountable in God's Word.

We start with a simple Bible reading plan, but it doesn't stop there.

Some gather in homes and churches locally, while others connect online with women across the globe. Whatever the method, we lovingly lock arms and unite for this purpose...

to Love God Greatly with our lives.

In today's fast-paced technology driven world, it would be easy to study God's Word in an isolated environment that lacks encouragement or support, but that isn't the intention here at Love God Greatly. God created us to live in community with Him and with those around us.

We need each other, and we live life better together.

Because of this, would you consider reaching out and studying with someone this session?

All of us have women in our lives who need friendship, accountability, and have the desire to dive into God's Word on a deeper level. Rest assured we'll be studying right alongside you - learning with you, cheering for you, enjoying sweet fellowship, and smiling from ear to ear as we watch God unite women together - intentionally connecting hearts and minds for His glory.

It's pretty unreal - this opportunity we have to not only grow closer to God through this study, but also to each other.

So here's the challenge: call your mom, your sister, your grandma, the girl across the street or the college friend across the country. Grab a group of girls from your church or workplace, or meet in a coffee shop with friends you have always wished you knew better. Utilize the beauty of connecting online for inspiration and accountability, and take opportunities to meet in person when you can.

Arm in arm and hand in hand,
let's do this thing... together.

We're proud of you.

We *really* want you to know that.

We're proud of you for making the commitment to be in God's Word… to be reading it each day and applying it to YOUR life - the beautiful life our Lord has given YOU.

Each session we offer a study journal that goes along with the verses we are reading. This journal is designed to help you interact with God's Word and learn to dig deeper - encouraging you to slow down to really reflect on what God is saying to you that day.

At *Love God Greatly*, we use the S.O.A.P. Bible study method. Before we begin, we'd like to take a moment to define this method and share WHY we recommend using it during your quiet time.

Why S.O.A.P. it?

It's one thing to simply read Scripture. But when you interact with it, intentionally slowing down to REALLY reflect on it, suddenly words start popping off the page. The SOAP method allows you to dig deeper into Scripture and see more than if you simply read the verses and then went on your merry way. We encourage you to take the time to S.O.A.P. through our Bible studies and see for yourself how much more you get out of your daily reading. You'll be amazed.

What does S.O.A.P. mean?

S- The S stands for Scripture. Physically write out the verses. You'll be amazed at what God will reveal to you just by taking the time to slow down and write out what you are reading!

O- The O stands for Observation. What do you see in the verses that you're reading? Who is the intended audience? Is there a repetition of words? What words stand out to you?

A- The A stands for Application. This is when God's Word becomes personal. What is God saying to me today? How can I apply what I just read to my own personal life? What changes do I need to make? Is there action that I need to take?

P- And finally, P stands for Prayer. Pray God's Word back to Him. Spend time thanking Him. If He has revealed something to you during this time in His Word, pray about it. If He has revealed some sin that is in your life, confess. And remember, He loves you dearly.

How To Soap

EXAMPLE: Read: Colossians 1:5-8

S- The faith and love that spring from the hope that is stored up for you in heaven and that you have already heard about in the word of truth, the gospel that has come to you. All over the world this gospel is bearing fruit and growing, just as it has been doing among you since the day you heard it and understood God's grace in all its truth. You learned it from Epaphras, our dear fellow servant, who is a faithful minister of Christ on our behalf, and who also told us of your love in the Spirit.

O-
- When you combine faith and love, you get hope.
- We have to remember that our hope is in heaven… it is yet to come.
- The gospel is the Word of Truth.
- The gospel is continually bearing fruit and growing from the first day to the last.
- It just takes one person to change a whole community… Epaphras.

A- God used one man, Epaphras, to change a whole town! I was reminded that we are simply called to tell others about Christ -it's God's job to spread the gospel, to grow it, and have it bear fruit. I felt today's verses were almost directly spoken to LGG… *"all over the world this gospel is bearing fruit and growing, just as it has been doing among you since the day you heard it and understood God's grace in all its truth."* It's so fun when God's Word becomes so alive and encourages us in our current situation! My passionate desire is that all the women involved in this Bible study will understand God's grace and have a thirst for His Word. Moved by this quote from my Bible commentary: ***"God's Word is not just for our information, it is for our transformation."***

P- Dear Lord, please help me to be an "Epaphras" - to tell others about You and then leave the results in Your loving hands. Please help me to understand and apply what I have read today to my life personally, thereby becoming more and more like You each and every day. Help me to live a life that bears the fruit of faith and love… anchoring my hope in heaven, not here on earth. Help me to remember that the BEST is yet to come!

Remember, the most important ingredients in the S.O.A.P. method are YOUR interaction with God's Word and your APPLICATION of His Word to YOUR life.

Blessed is the man whose *"delight is in the law of the Lord, and on his law he meditates day and night. He is like a tree planted by streams of water, which yields its fruit in season and whose leaf does not wither. Whatever he does prospers."* ~ Psalm 1:2-3

Soap Reading Plan

		Read	SOAP
WEEK 1	Monday	Acts 2:41-47	Acts 2:42
	Tuesday	Hebrews 4:15-16	Hebrews 4:16
	Wednesday	Jeremiah 10:6-7	Jeremiah 10:6-7
	Thursday	Psalm 145:1-7	Psalm 145:1-2
	Friday	Romans 15:30; Colossians 1:9	Colossians 1:9
	Response Day		
WEEK 2	Monday	1 Timothy 2:8	1 Timothy 2:8
	Tuesday	Mark 1:35; Matthew 14:23	Mark 1:35
	Wednesday	Acts 9:40	Acts 9:40
	Thursday	Ephesians 3:14-16	Ephesians 3:14-16
	Friday	John 15:1-5	John 15:5
	Response Day		
WEEK 3	Monday	Psalm 145:1-13	Psalm 145:1-3
	Tuesday	Isaiah 6:1-6	Isaiah 6:5
	Wednesday	Philippians 4:5–7	Philippians 4:6
	Thursday	Hebrews 13:15	Hebrews 13:15
	Friday	Psalm 140	Psalm 140:9-11
	Response Day		
WEEK 4	Monday	Psalm 62	Psalm 62:8
	Tuesday	Psalm 37:7-8	Psalm 37:7-8
	Wednesday	Luke 18:1-7	Luke 18:1,7
	Thursday	Mark 11:23-24	Mark 11:24
	Friday	Colossians 4:2; 1 Thessalonians 5:17	1 Thessalonians 5:17
	Response Day		
WEEK 5	Monday	Ephesians 1:15-18	Ephesians 1:17
	Tuesday	Matthew 26:40-41	Matthew 26:41
	Wednesday	Colossians 1:3-12	Colossians 1:3-4
	Thursday	1 Timothy 2:1-3	1 Timothy 2:1-2
	Friday	Luke 6:27-28	Luke 6:27-28
	Response Day		
WEEK 6	Monday	Romans 5:1-2	Romans 5:2
	Tuesday	1 John 5:13-15	1 John 5:14
	Wednesday	Isaiah 41:10; Psalm 34:18	Psalm 34:18
	Thursday	Matthew 7:7-11	Matthew 7:11
	Friday	Romans 8:26-27	Romans 8:27
	Response Day		
WEEK 7	Monday	2 Corinthians 12:7-10	2 Corinthians 12:8-9
	Tuesday	1 Samuel 1:1-20	1 Samuel 1:20
	Wednesday	Psalm 37:7; Lamentations 3:25	Psalm 37:7
	Thursday	1 Kings 18:20-39	1 Kings 18:38-39
	Friday	John 1:16; Ephesians 3:20-21	John 1:16; Ephesians 3:20
	Response Day		
WEEK 8	Monday	Psalm 5:3; Proverbs 8:17	Psalm 5:3
	Tuesday	Psalm 63:5-8	Psalm 63:5-6
	Wednesday	Psalm 100	Psalm 100:4-5
	Thursday	Psalm 18:1-6	Psalm 18:6
	Friday	Psalm 51	Psalm 51:2-4
	Response Day		

Goals

We believe it's important to write out goals for each session. Take some time now and write three goals you would like to focus on this session as we begin to rise each day and dig into God's Word. Make sure and refer back to these goals throughout the next eight weeks to help you stay focused. YOU CAN DO IT!!!

My goals for this session are:

1.

2.

3.

Signature: _____

Date: _____

Intro To Prayer

Prayer is the spiritual pulse: by this,
the spiritual health may always be tested.

J.C. Ryle (1816-1900)

I'm going to be totally honest. Prayer is the easiest and the hardest discipline for me. It is easy in that it does not require I have any special talents, sophisticated vocabulary, or a specific place I need to go. And yet it is difficult because I am easily distracted, lacking in faithfulness, and ignorant to the dangers of a prayerless life.

Anyone else have these struggles?

Prayer is a privilege that we take for granted, and a discipline many find boring. It is a gift that we don't value or always believe in. And yet, in our most desperate times what do we do? We pray, almost as if it is instinctive.

From Adam and Eve to the Apostle John, prayer is found throughout the entire counsel of God. Most of us know prayer is speaking to God, but it's so much more than that. It is communion with God - the experience of fellowship that allows us to draw near to Him and find help when we need it.

The Privilege of Prayer

To be able to draw near to God, anytime and anywhere, is a humbling privilege. As sinners, we do not deserve to have any access to Him. Who is God? Infinite in holiness, perfection, righteousness and purity. Who are we? Created creatures, full of pride, dead in our trespasses and sin. We are not worthy to enter into His presence, let alone speak directly to the Almighty One.

But there is One who is able to set all things right. Jesus, whose name means, "The Lord Saves," came to reconcile us to God through His death and resurrection. He took upon Himself our punishment; He paid our ransom so that, through faith, we could be made right with God.

We are now saved by grace, adopted children of the Father, and co-heirs with Christ. This means that we now belong in the presence of God. Our vileness has been covered with the righteous robe of Jesus. Therefore, we have complete access to the throne room of the Almighty before whom even the angels cover their eyes (Is. 6:2; Rev. 4:8). Along with entering into the presence of God through prayer, we also have His full and loving attention. We have access to the ear of God, and this is critically important to the life of faith.

Growing through prayer

The reason so many of us are slow to pray is because we do not believe prayer is important. We think we can make it through our day without the help and guidance of God. We act as though we are resolute enough to resist temptation, strong enough to fight the attacks of Satan, savvy enough to navigate the ways of the world, and spiritual enough to figure out the word of God on our own. We believe that we are self-sufficient.

When looking at the life of Jesus, one thing we can't help but see are the number of times He withdraws from the people to spend time with His Father in prayer (Mark 1:35; Matt. 14:23; Luke 6:12; Luke 22.32). The Son of God who calmed storms, banished devils, and overcame sickness, knew the importance of prayer and made it a part of His daily life.

Prayer is the most important subject in practical religion. All other subjects are second to it. Reading the Bible, keeping the Sabbath, hearing sermons, attending public worship, going to the Lord's Table—all these are very weighty matters. But none of them is as important as private prayer.

J. C. Ryle (1816-1900)

Prayer is important because …

It refocuses our eyes on Jesus.
It gives us strength.
It draws us close to God.
It brings comfort.
It produces peace.
It ignites love for God.
It is a place of refuge during times of sorrow and pain.
It is a place of healing for the battered and hurt.
It is a time to seek clarity and wisdom.
It is a time of praise and worship.

Prayer is important, but it isn't God who needs it. God does not need our prayers, but He has chosen to work through them, to heal, restore, motivate, sooth, and save.

Intro To Prayer

Ah! How often, Christians, hath God kissed you at the beginning of prayer, and spoken peace to you in the midst of prayer, and filled you with joy and assurance upon the close of prayer!

Thomas Brooks (1608-1680)

Join us in our study as we seek to answer questions like, "How should we pray?" "What should we pray for?" "Does God hear our prayers?"

My prayer is that the knowledge received through our study will be transformed into the fuel we need to become women marked by prayer - that it would, as Robert L. Dabney said, be our "vital breath."

Week 1 Challenge (Note: You can find this listed in our Monday blog post):

Prayer focus for this week: Spend time praying for your family members.

	Praying	*Praise*
Monday		
Tuesday		
Wednesday		
Thursday		
Friday		

Let us then with
confidence draw near
To the Throne of grace,
That we may
receive mercy and find grace
To help in time of need.

Hebrews 4:16

Week 1

SCRIPTURE FOR THIS WEEK

Acts 2:41-47 ESV

⁴¹ So those who received his word were baptized, and there were added that day about three thousand souls. ⁴² And they devoted themselves to the apostles' teaching and the fellowship, to the breaking of bread and the prayers. ⁴³ And awe came upon every soul, and many wonders and signs were being done through the apostles. ⁴⁴ And all who believed were together and had all things in common. ⁴⁵ And they were selling their possessions and belongings and distributing the proceeds to all, as any had need. ⁴⁶ And day by day, attending the temple together and breaking bread in their homes, they received their food with glad and generous hearts, ⁴⁷ praising God and having favor with all the people. And the Lord added to their number day by day those who were being saved.

Hebrews 4:15-16 ESV

¹⁵ For we do not have a high priest who is unable to sympathize with our weaknesses, but one who in every respect has been tempted as we are, yet without sin. ¹⁶ Let us then with confidence draw near to the throne of grace, that we may receive mercy and find grace to help in time of need.

Jeremiah 10:6-7 ESV

⁶ There is none like you, O Lord; you are great, and your name is great in might. ⁷ Who would not fear you, O King of the nations? For this is your due; for among all the wise ones of the nations and in all their kingdoms there is none like you.

Week 1
SCRIPTURE FOR THIS WEEK

Psalm 145:1-7 ESV

I will extol you, my God and King, and bless your name forever and ever. [2] Every day I will bless you and praise your name forever and ever. [3] Great is the Lord, and greatly to be praised, and his greatness is unsearchable.

[4] One generation shall commend your works to another, and shall declare your mighty acts. [5] On the glorious splendor of your majesty, and on your wondrous works, I will meditate. [6] They shall speak of the might of your awesome deeds, and I will declare your greatness. [7] They shall pour forth the fame of your abundant goodness and shall sing aloud of your righteousness.

Romans 15:30 ESV

[30] I appeal to you, brothers, by our Lord Jesus Christ and by the love of the Spirit, to strive together with me in your prayers to God on my behalf.

Colossians 1:9 ESV

[9] And so, from the day we heard, we have not ceased to pray for you, asking that you may be filled with the knowledge of his will in all spiritual wisdom and understanding,

Read: Acts 2:41-47
Soap: Acts 2:42

Scripture - Write out the **Scripture** passage for the day.

Observations - Write down 1 or 2 **observations** from the passage.

Monday

Applications - Write down 1 or 2 **applications** from the passage.

Pray - Write out a **prayer** over what you learned from today's passage.

Read: Hebrews 4:15-16
Soap: Hebrews 4:16

Scripture - Write out the **Scripture** passage for the day.

Observations - Write down 1 or 2 **observations** from the passage.

Applications - Write down 1 or 2 **applications** from the passage.

Pray - Write out a **prayer** over what you learned from today's passage.

Read: Jeremiah 10:6-7
Soap: Jeremiah 10:6-7

Scripture - Write out the **Scripture** passage for the day.

Observations - Write down 1 or 2 **observations** from the passage.

Applications - Write down 1 or 2 **applications** from the passage.

Pray - Write out a **prayer** over what you learned from today's passage.

Thursday

Read: Psalm 145:1-7
Soap: Psalm 145:1-2

Scripture - Write out the **Scripture** passage for the day.

Observations - Write down 1 or 2 **observations** from the passage.

Thursday

Applications - Write down 1 or 2 **applications** from the passage.

Pray - Write out a **prayer** over what you learned from today's passage.

Read: Romans 15:30; Colossians 1:9
Soap: Colossians 1:9

Scripture - Write out the **Scripture** passage for the day.

Observations - Write down 1 or 2 **observations** from the passage.

Friday

Applications - Write down 1 or 2 **applications** from the passage.

Pray - Write out a **prayer** over what you learned from today's passage.

-Visit our website today for the corresponding blog post!-

Reflection Questions

1. Write your own definition of prayer.

2. Why is prayer such a gift to God's people?

3. J.C. Ryle said that praying is the most important thing a Christian can do. He said, "Prayer is to faith what breath is to life. How a man can live and not breathe is past my comprehension, and how a man can believe and not pray is past my comprehension too." Do you agree? Why or why not.

4. What does prayer teach us about God?

5. We are told to pray for each other. Find another verse that also teaches us to pray for other believers.

My Response

WEEK 1

Week 2 Challenge (Note: You can find this listed in our Monday blog post):

Prayer focus for this week: Spend time praying for your country.

	Praying	*Praise*
Monday		
Tuesday		
Wednesday		
Thursday		
Friday		

And rising very early in the morning, while it was still dark, he departed and went out to a desolate place, and there he prayed.

Mark 1:35

Week 2
SCRIPTURE FOR THIS WEEK

1 Timothy 2:8 ESV

8 I desire then that in every place the men should pray, lifting holy hands without anger or quarreling;

Mark 1:35 ESV

35 And rising very early in the morning, while it was still dark, he departed and went out to a desolate place, and there he prayed.

Matthew 14:23 ESV

23 And after he had dismissed the crowds, he went up on the mountain by himself to pray. When evening came, he was there alone,

Acts 9:40 ESV

40 But Peter put them all outside, and knelt down and prayed; and turning to the body he said, "Tabitha, arise." And she opened her eyes, and when she saw Peter she sat up.

Ephesians 3:14-16 ESV

14 For this reason I bow my knees before the Father, 15 from whom every family in heaven and on earth is named, 16 that according to the riches of his glory he may grant you to be strengthened with power through his Spirit in your inner being,

SCRIPTURE FOR THIS WEEK

John 15:1-5 ESV

"I am the true vine, and my Father is the vinedresser. [2] Every branch in me that does not bear fruit he takes away, and every branch that does bear fruit he prunes, that it may bear more fruit. [3] Already you are clean because of the word that I have spoken to you. [4] Abide in me, and I in you. As the branch cannot bear fruit by itself, unless it abides in the vine, neither can you, unless you abide in me. [5] I am the vine; you are the branches. Whoever abides in me and I in him, he it is that bears much fruit, for apart from me you can do nothing.

Read: 1 Timothy 2:8
Soap: 1 Timothy 2:8

Scripture - Write out the **Scripture** passage for the day.

Observations - Write down 1 or 2 **observations** from the passage.

Monday

Applications - Write down 1 or 2 **applications** from the passage.

Pray - Write out a **prayer** over what you learned from today's passage.

Tuesday

Read: Mark 1:35; Matthew 14:23
Soap: Mark 1:35

Scripture - Write out the **Scripture** passage for the day.

Observations - Write down 1 or 2 **observations** from the passage.

Tuesday

Applications - Write down 1 or 2 **applications** from the passage.

Pray - Write out a **prayer** over what you learned from today's passage.

Read: Acts 9:40
Soap: Acts 9:40

Scripture - Write out the **Scripture** passage for the day.

Observations - Write down 1 or 2 **observations** from the passage.

Wednesday

Applications - Write down 1 or 2 **applications** from the passage.

Pray - Write out a **prayer** over what you learned from today's passage.

-Visit our website today for the corresponding blog post!-

Read: Ephesians 3:14-16
Soap: Ephesians 3:14-16

Scripture - Write out the **Scripture** passage for the day.

Observations - Write down 1 or 2 **observations** from the passage.

Thursday

Applications - Write down 1 or 2 **applications** from the passage.

Pray - Write out a **prayer** over what you learned from today's passage.

Read: John 15:1-5
Soap: John 15:5

Scripture - Write out the **Scripture** passage for the day.

Observations - Write down 1 or 2 **observations** from the passage.

Friday

Applications - Write down 1 or 2 **applications** from the passage.

Pray - Write out a **prayer** over what you learned from today's passage.

-Visit our website today for the corresponding blog post!-

Reflection Questions

1. How does pride affect our prayer life?

2. Read Luke 17:6. What do you think Jesus means in this verse?

3. How does prayer give us strength?

4. Write down your favorite verse on prayer.

5. We are totally dependent on God for all things. How does prayer help to remind us of this truth?

My Response

Week 3 Challenge (Note: You can find this listed in our Monday blog post):

Prayer focus for this week: Spend time praying for your friends.

	Praying	Praise
Monday		
Tuesday		
Wednesday		
Thursday		
Friday		

Through Him
Then let us
continually
offer up a
sacrifice of praise
to God,
That is, The
fruit of lips
That acknowledge
his name.

Hebrews 13:15

Psalm 145:1-13 ESV

I will extol you, my God and King, and bless your name forever and ever. [2] Every day I will bless you and praise your name forever and ever. [3] Great is the Lord, and greatly to be praised, and his greatness is unsearchable.

[4] One generation shall commend your works to another, and shall declare your mighty acts. [5] On the glorious splendor of your majesty, and on your wondrous works, I will meditate. [6] They shall speak of the might of your awesome deeds, and I will declare your greatness. [7] They shall pour forth the fame of your abundant goodness and shall sing aloud of your righteousness.

[8] The Lord is gracious and merciful, slow to anger and abounding in steadfast love. [9] The Lord is good to all, and his mercy is over all that he has made.

[10] All your works shall give thanks to you, O Lord, and all your saints shall bless you! [11] They shall speak of the glory of your kingdom and tell of your power, [12] to make known to the children of man your mighty deeds, and the glorious splendor of your kingdom. [13] Your kingdom is an everlasting kingdom, and your dominion endures throughout all generations. [The Lord is faithful in all his words and kind in all his works.]

Isaiah 6:1-6 ESV

In the year that King Uzziah died I saw the Lord sitting upon a throne, high and lifted up; and the train of his robe filled the temple. [2] Above him stood the seraphim. Each had six wings: with two he covered his face, and with two he covered his feet, and with two he flew. [3] And one called to another and said: "Holy, holy, holy is the Lord of hosts; the whole earth is full of his glory!"

[4] And the foundations of the thresholds shook at the voice of him who called, and the house was filled with smoke. [5] And I said: "Woe is me! For I am lost; for I am a man of unclean lips, and I dwell in the midst of a people of unclean lips; for my eyes have seen the King, the Lord of hosts!" [6] Then one of the seraphim flew to me, having in his hand a burning coal that he had taken with tongs from the altar.

Week 3

SCRIPTURE FOR THIS WEEK

Philippians 4:5-7 ESV

⁵ Let your reasonableness be known to everyone. The Lord is at hand; ⁶ do not be anxious about anything, but in everything by prayer and supplication with thanksgiving let your requests be made known to God. ⁷ And the peace of God, which surpasses all understanding, will guard your hearts and your minds in Christ Jesus.

Hebrews 13:15 ESV

¹⁵ Through him then let us continually offer up a sacrifice of praise to God, that is, the fruit of lips that acknowledge his name.

Psalm 140 ESV

Deliver me, O Lord, from evil men; preserve me from violent men, ² who plan evil things in their heart and stir up wars continually. ³ They make their tongue sharp as a serpent's, and under their lips is the venom of asps.

⁴ Guard me, O Lord, from the hands of the wicked; preserve me from violent men, who have planned to trip up my feet. ⁵ The arrogant have hidden a trap for me, and with cords they have spread a net; beside the way they have set snares for me.

⁶ I say to the Lord, You are my God; give ear to the voice of my pleas for mercy, O Lord! ⁷ O Lord, my Lord, the strength of my salvation, you have covered my head in the day of battle. ⁸ Grant not, O Lord, the desires of the wicked; do not further their[b] evil plot, or they will be exalted!

⁹ As for the head of those who surround me, let the mischief of their lips overwhelm them! ¹⁰ Let burning coals fall upon them! Let them be cast into fire, into miry pits, no more to rise! ¹¹ Let not the slanderer be established in the land; let evil hunt down the violent man speedily!

¹² I know that the Lord will maintain the cause of the afflicted, and will execute justice for the needy. ¹³ Surely the righteous shall give thanks to your name; the upright shall dwell in your presence.

Read: Psalm 145:1-13
Soap: Psalm 145:1-3

Scripture - Write out the **Scripture** passage for the day.

Observations - Write down 1 or 2 **observations** from the passage.

Applications - Write down 1 or 2 **applications** from the passage.

Pray - Write out a **prayer** over what you learned from today's passage.

Read: Isaiah 6:1-6
Soap: Isaiah 6:5

Scripture - Write out the **Scripture** passage for the day.

Observations - Write down 1 or 2 **observations** from the passage.

Tuesday

Applications - Write down 1 or 2 **applications** from the passage.

Pray - Write out a **prayer** over what you learned from today's passage.

Read: Philippians 4:5-7
Soap: Philippians 4:6

Scripture - Write out the **Scripture** passage for the day.

Observations - Write down 1 or 2 **observations** from the passage.

Wednesday

Applications - Write down 1 or 2 **applications** from the passage.

Pray - Write out a **prayer** over what you learned from today's passage.

Read: Hebrews 13:15
Soap: Hebrews 13:15

Scripture - Write out the **Scripture** passage for the day.

Observations - Write down 1 or 2 **observations** from the passage.

Thursday

Applications - Write down 1 or 2 **applications** from the passage.

Pray - Write out a **prayer** over what you learned from today's passage.

Friday

Read: Psalm 140
Soap: Psalm 140:9-11

Scripture - Write out the **Scripture** passage for the day.

Observations - Write down 1 or 2 **observations** from the passage.

Applications - Write down 1 or 2 **applications** from the passage.

Pray - Write out a **prayer** over what you learned from today's passage.

Reflection Questions

1. What are some attributes of God that you can talk about in your time of adoration?

2. Ephesians 6:18 tells us to "pray at all times and on every occasion." How is this possible in real life?

3. How can we get away from our prayers turning into a shopping list of requests?

4. How can we learn to be truly thankful for all things?

5. Do some research on imprecatory prayers. Should we still use these kinds of prayers today?

My Response

WEEK 3

Week 4 Challenge (Note: You can find this listed in our Monday blog post):

Prayer focus for this week: Spend time praying for your church.

	Praying	Praise
Monday		
Tuesday		
Wednesday		
Thursday		
Friday		

And he told them a parable to the effect that they ought always to pray and not lose heart.

Luke 18:1

SCRIPTURE FOR THIS WEEK

Psalm 62 ESV

For God alone my soul waits in silence; from him comes my salvation. [2] He alone is my rock and my salvation, my fortress; I shall not be greatly shaken.

[3] How long will all of you attack a man to batter him, like a leaning wall, a tottering fence? [4] They only plan to thrust him down from his high position. They take pleasure in falsehood. They bless with their mouths, but inwardly they curse.

[5] For God alone, O my soul, wait in silence, for my hope is from him. [6] He only is my rock and my salvation, my fortress; I shall not be shaken. [7] On God rests my salvation and my glory; my mighty rock, my refuge is God.

[8] Trust in him at all times, O people; pour out your heart before him; God is a refuge for us.

[9] Those of low estate are but a breath; those of high estate are a delusion; in the balances they go up; they are together lighter than a breath. [10] Put no trust in extortion; set no vain hopes on robbery; if riches increase, set not your heart on them.

[11] Once God has spoken; twice have I heard this: that power belongs to God, [12] and that to you, O Lord, belongs steadfast love. For you will render to a man according to his work.

Psalm 37:7-8 ESV

[7] Be still before the Lord and wait patiently for him; fret not yourself over the one who prospers in his way, over the man who carries out evil devices!

[8] Refrain from anger, and forsake wrath! Fret not yourself; it tends only to evil.

Luke 18:1-7 ESV

And he told them a parable to the effect that they ought always to pray and not lose heart. [2] He said, "In a certain city there was a judge who neither feared God nor respected man. [3] And there was a widow in that city who kept coming to him and saying, 'Give me justice against my adversary.'

[4] For a while he refused, but afterward he said to himself, 'Though I neither fear God nor respect man, [5] yet because this widow keeps bothering me, I will give her justice, so that she will not beat me down by her continual coming.'" [6] And the Lord said, "Hear what the unrighteous judge says. [7] And will not God give justice to his elect, who cry to him day and night? Will he delay long over them?

Mark 11:23-24 ESV

[23] Truly, I say to you, whoever says to this mountain, 'Be taken up and thrown into the sea,' and does not doubt in his heart, but believes that what he says will come to pass, it will be done for him. [24] Therefore I tell you, whatever you ask in prayer, believe that you have received it, and it will be yours.

Colossians 4:2 ESV

[2] Continue steadfastly in prayer, being watchful in it with thanksgiving.

1 Thessalonians 5:17 ESV

[17] pray without ceasing,

Read: Psalm 62
Soap: Psalm 62:8

Scripture - Write out the **Scripture** passage for the day.

Observations - Write down 1 or 2 **observations** from the passage.

Applications - Write down 1 or 2 **applications** from the passage.

Pray - Write out a **prayer** over what you learned from today's passage.

Read: Psalm 37:7-8
Soap: Psalm 37:7-8

Scripture - Write out the **Scripture** passage for the day.

Observations - Write down 1 or 2 **observations** from the passage.

Tuesday

Applications - Write down 1 or 2 **applications** from the passage.

Pray - Write out a **prayer** over what you learned from today's passage.

Read: Luke 18:1-7
Soap: Luke 18:1, 7

Scripture - Write out the **Scripture** passage for the day.

Observations - Write down 1 or 2 **observations** from the passage.

Wednesday

Applications - Write down 1 or 2 **applications** from the passage.

Pray - Write out a **prayer** over what you learned from today's passage.

Thursday

Read: Mark 11:23-24
Soap: Mark 11:24

Scripture - Write out the **Scripture** passage for the day.

Observations - Write down 1 or 2 **observations** from the passage.

Thursday

Applications - Write down 1 or 2 **applications** from the passage.

Pray - Write out a **prayer** over what you learned from today's passage.

Friday

Read: Colossians 4:2; 1 Thessalonians 5:17
Soap: 1 Thessalonians 5:17

Scripture - Write out the **Scripture** passage for the day.

Observations - Write down 1 or 2 **observations** from the passage.

Friday

Applications - Write down 1 or 2 **applications** from the passage.

Pray - Write out a **prayer** over what you learned from today's passage.

-Visit our website today for the corresponding blog post!-

Reflection Questions

1. Is there a proper way to pray?

2. Why is patience so important in our prayer life?

3. How should boldness affect our prayers?

4. What is the difference between prayers uttered in faith and those prayed with doubt?

5. Write out anything new you have learned this week.

My Response

WEEK 4

Week 5 Challenge (Note: You can find this listed in our Monday blog post):

Prayer focus for this week: Spend time praying for missionaries.

	Praying	*Praise*
Monday		
Tuesday		
Wednesday		
Thursday		
Friday		

LoveGodGreatly.com

But I say to you who hear,
love your enemies,
do good to those who
hate you,
bless those who
curse you,
pray for those who
abuse you.

Luke 6:27-28

SCRIPTURE FOR THIS WEEK

Ephesians 1:15-18 ESV

[15] For this reason, because I have heard of your faith in the Lord Jesus and your love toward all the saints, [16] I do not cease to give thanks for you, remembering you in my prayers, [17] that the God of our Lord Jesus Christ, the Father of glory, may give you the Spirit of wisdom and of revelation in the knowledge of him, [18] having the eyes of your hearts enlightened, that you may know what is the hope to which he has called you, what are the riches of his glorious inheritance in the saints,

Matthew 26:40-41 ESV

[40] And he came to the disciples and found them sleeping. And he said to Peter, "So, could you not watch with me one hour? [41] Watch and pray that you may not enter into temptation. The spirit indeed is willing, but the flesh is weak."

Colossians 1:3-12 ESV

[3] We always thank God, the Father of our Lord Jesus Christ, when we pray for you, [4] since we heard of your faith in Christ Jesus and of the love that you have for all the saints, [5] because of the hope laid up for you in heaven. Of this you have heard before in the word of the truth, the gospel, [6] which has come to you, as indeed in the whole world it is bearing fruit and increasing—as it also does among you, since the day you heard it and understood the grace of God in truth, [7] just as you learned it from Epaphras our beloved fellow servant. He is a faithful minister of Christ on your behalf [8] and has made known to us your love in the Spirit.

[9] And so, from the day we heard, we have not ceased to pray for you, asking that you may be filled with the knowledge of his will in all spiritual wisdom and understanding, [10] so as to walk in a manner worthy of the Lord, fully pleasing to him, bearing fruit in every good work and increasing in the knowledge of God. [11] May you be strengthened with all power, according to

his glorious might, for all endurance and patience with joy, [12] giving thanks to the Father, who has qualified you[e] to share in the inheritance of the saints in light.

1 Timothy 2:1-3 ESV

First of all, then, I urge that supplications, prayers, intercessions, and thanksgivings be made for all people, ² for kings and all who are in high positions, that we may lead a peaceful and quiet life, godly and dignified in every way. ³ This is good, and it is pleasing in the sight of God our Savior,

Luke 6:27-28 ESV

²⁷ "But I say to you who hear, Love your enemies, do good to those who hate you, ²⁸ bless those who curse you, pray for those who abuse you.

Monday

Read: Ephesians 1:15-18
Soap: Ephesians 1:17

Scripture - Write out the **Scripture** passage for the day.

Observations - Write down 1 or 2 **observations** from the passage.

Applications - Write down 1 or 2 **applications** from the passage.

Pray - Write out a **prayer** over what you learned from today's passage.

Read: Matthew 26:40-41
Soap: Matthew 26:41

Scripture - Write out the **Scripture** passage for the day.

Observations - Write down 1 or 2 **observations** from the passage.

Applications - Write down 1 or 2 **applications** from the passage.

Pray - Write out a **prayer** over what you learned from today's passage.

Read: Colossians 1:3-12
Soap: Colossians 1:3-4

Scripture - Write out the **Scripture** passage for the day.

Observations - Write down 1 or 2 **observations** from the passage.

Wednesday

Applications - Write down 1 or 2 **applications** from the passage.

Pray - Write out a **prayer** over what you learned from today's passage.

Read: 1 Timothy 2:1-3
Soap: 1 Timothy 2:1-2

Scripture - Write out the **Scripture** passage for the day.

Observations - Write down 1 or 2 **observations** from the passage.

Thursday

Applications - Write down 1 or 2 **applications** from the passage.

Pray - Write out a **prayer** over what you learned from today's passage.

Read: Luke 6:27-28
Soap: Luke 6:27-28

Scripture - Write out the **Scripture** passage for the day.

Observations - Write down 1 or 2 **observations** from the passage.

Friday

Applications
- Write down 1 or 2 **applications** from the passage.

Pray
- Write out a **prayer** over what you learned from today's passage.

-Visit our website today for the corresponding blog post!-

Reflection Questions

1. Many of our prayers revolve around our physical needs. What spiritual needs should we pray for?

2. How can prayer help during times of temptation?

3. Write out a prayer for a fellow believer (you don't have to share this with them, though you could let them know that you prayed for them).

4. James 4:3 says, "You ask and do not receive, because you ask wrongly, to spend it on your passion". What does he mean when he said "you ask wrongly?"

5. What is the hardest part about praying for our enemies?

My Response

WEEK 5

Week 6

Week 6 Challenge (Note: You can find this listed in our Monday blog post):

Prayer focus for this week: Spend time praying for you.

	Praying	Praise
Monday		
Tuesday		
Wednesday		
Thursday		
Friday		

LoveGodGreatly.com

And This is The confidence That we have Toward him, That if we ask anything according To his will he hears us.

1 John 5:14

Week 6

SCRIPTURE FOR THIS WEEK

Romans 5:1-2 ESV

Therefore, since we have been justified by faith, we have peace with God through our Lord Jesus Christ. ² Through him we have also obtained access by faith into this grace in which we stand, and we rejoice in hope of the glory of God.

1 John 5:13-15 ESV

¹³ I write these things to you who believe in the name of the Son of God that you may know that you have eternal life. ¹⁴ And this is the confidence that we have toward him, that if we ask anything according to his will he hears us. ¹⁵ And if we know that he hears us in whatever we ask, we know that we have the requests that we have asked of him.

Isaiah. 41:10 ESV

¹⁰ fear not, for I am with you; be not dismayed, for I am your God; I will strengthen you, I will help you, I will uphold you with my righteous right hand.

Psalm 34:18 ESV

¹⁸ The Lord is near to the brokenhearted and saves the crushed in spirit.

Matthew 7:7-11 ESV

⁷ "Ask, and it will be given to you; seek, and you will find; knock, and it will be opened to you. ⁸ For everyone who asks receives, and the one who seeks finds, and to the one who knocks it will be opened. ⁹ Or which one of you, if his son asks him for bread, will give him a stone? ¹⁰ Or if he asks for a fish, will give him a serpent? ¹¹ If you then, who are evil, know how to give good gifts to your children, how much more will your Father who is in heaven give good things to those who ask him!

Week 6

SCRIPTURE FOR THIS WEEK

Romans 8:26-27 ESV

²⁶ Likewise the Spirit helps us in our weakness. For we do not know what to pray for as we ought, but the Spirit himself intercedes for us with groanings too deep for words. ²⁷ And he who searches hearts knows what is the mind of the Spirit, because the Spirit intercedes for the saints according to the will of God.

Read: Romans 5:1-2
Soap: Romans 5:2

Scripture - Write out the **Scripture** passage for the day.

Observations - Write down 1 or 2 **observations** from the passage.

Monday

Applications - Write down 1 or 2 **applications** from the passage.

Pray - Write out a **prayer** over what you learned from today's passage.

Tuesday

Read: 1 John 5:13-15
Soap: 1 John 5:14

Scripture - Write out the **Scripture** passage for the day.

Observations - Write down 1 or 2 **observations** from the passage.

Applications - Write down 1 or 2 **applications** from the passage.

Pray - Write out a **prayer** over what you learned from today's passage.

Wednesday

Read: Isaiah. 41:10; Psalm 34:18
Soap: Psalm 34:18

Scripture - Write out the **Scripture** passage for the day.

Observations - Write down 1 or 2 **observations** from the passage.

Wednesday

Applications - Write down 1 or 2 **applications** from the passage.

Pray - Write out a **prayer** over what you learned from today's passage.

-Visit our website today for the corresponding blog post!-

Read: Matthew 7:7-11
Soap: Matthew 7:11

Scripture - Write out the **Scripture** passage for the day.

Observations - Write down 1 or 2 **observations** from the passage.

Applications - Write down 1 or 2 **applications** from the passage.

Pray - Write out a **prayer** over what you learned from today's passage.

Read: Romans 8:26-27
Soap: Romans 8:27

Scripture - Write out the **Scripture** passage for the day.

Observations - Write down 1 or 2 **observations** from the passage.

Applications - Write down 1 or 2 **applications** from the passage.

Pray - Write out a **prayer** over what you learned from today's passage.

-Visit our website today for the corresponding blog post!-

Reflection Questions

1. How can we as sinners approach God for anything?

2. God no longer relates to us as judge, but as Father. How should this knowledge affect our prayer life?

3. What does it mean for God to be close (Psalm 34:11)?

4. What is the Holy Spirit's job in regard to our prayers?

5. Read Romans 8:26. Explain what this verse is talking about.

My Response

WEEK 6

Week 7 Challenge (Note: You can find this listed in our Monday blog post):

Prayer focus for this week: Spend time this week turning your fears into prayers.

	Praying	Praise
Monday		
Tuesday		
Wednesday		
Thursday		
Friday		

Now to him
who is able to do
far more
abundantly
than all that
we ask or think,
according to the
power at work
within us,

Ephesians 3:20

SCRIPTURE FOR THIS WEEK

2 Corinthians 12:7-10 ESV

[7] So to keep me from becoming conceited because of the surpassing greatness of the revelations, a thorn was given me in the flesh, a messenger of Satan to harass me, to keep me from becoming conceited. [8] Three times I pleaded with the Lord about this, that it should leave me. [9] But he said to me, "My grace is sufficient for you, for my power is made perfect in weakness." Therefore I will boast all the more gladly of my weaknesses, so that the power of Christ may rest upon me. [10] For the sake of Christ, then, I am content with weaknesses, insults, hardships, persecutions, and calamities. For when I am weak, then I am strong.

1 Samuel 1:1-20 ESV

There was a certain man of Ramathaim-zophim of the hill country of Ephraim whose name was Elkanah the son of Jeroham, son of Elihu, son of Tohu, son of Zuph, an Ephrathite. [2] He had two wives. The name of the one was Hannah, and the name of the other, Peninnah. And Peninnah had children, but Hannah had no children.

[3] Now this man used to go up year by year from his city to worship and to sacrifice to the Lord of hosts at Shiloh, where the two sons of Eli, Hophni and Phinehas, were priests of the Lord. [4] On the day when Elkanah sacrificed, he would give portions to Peninnah his wife and to all her sons and daughters. [5] But to Hannah he gave a double portion, because he loved her, though the Lord had closed her womb. [6] And her rival used to provoke her grievously to irritate her, because the Lord had closed her womb. [7] So it went on year by year. As often as she went up to the house of the Lord, she used to provoke her. Therefore Hannah wept and would not eat. [8] And Elkanah, her husband, said to her, "Hannah, why do you weep? And why do you not eat? And why is your heart sad? Am I not more to you than ten sons?"

[9] After they had eaten and drunk in Shiloh, Hannah rose. Now Eli the priest was sitting on the seat beside the doorpost of the temple of the Lord. [10] She was deeply distressed and prayed to the Lord and wept bitterly. [11] And she vowed a vow and said, "O Lord of hosts, if you will indeed look on the affliction of your servant and remember me and not forget your servant, but will give to your servant a son, then I will give him to the Lord all the days of his life, and no razor shall touch his head."

[12] As she continued praying before the Lord, Eli observed her mouth. [13] Hannah was speaking in her heart; only her lips moved, and her voice was not heard. Therefore Eli took her to be a drunken woman. [14] And Eli said to her, "How long will you go on being drunk? Put your wine away from you." [15] But Hannah answered, "No, my lord, I am a woman troubled in spirit. I have drunk neither wine nor strong drink, but I have been pouring out my soul before the Lord. [16] Do not regard your servant as a worthless woman, for all along I have been speaking out of my great anxiety and vexation." [17] Then Eli answered, "Go in peace, and the God of Israel grant your petition that you have made to him." [18] And she said, "Let your servant find favor in your eyes." Then the woman went her way and ate, and her face was no longer sad.

[19] They rose early in the morning and worshiped before the Lord; then they went back to their house at Ramah. And Elkanah knew Hannah his wife, and the Lord remembered her. [20] And in due time Hannah conceived and bore a son, and she called his name Samuel, for she said, "I have asked for him from the Lord."

Psalm 37:7 ESV

[7] Be still before the Lord and wait patiently for him; fret not yourself over the one who prospers in his way, over the man who carries out evil devices!

Lamentations 3:25 ESV

[25] The Lord is good to those who wait for him, to the soul who seeks him.

1 Kings 18:20-39 ESV

²⁰ So Ahab sent to all the people of Israel and gathered the prophets together at Mount Carmel. ²¹ And Elijah came near to all the people and said, "How long will you go limping between two different opinions? If the Lord is God, follow him; but if Baal, then follow him." And the people did not answer him a word. ²² Then Elijah said to the people, "I, even I only, am left a prophet of the Lord, but Baal's prophets are 450 men. ²³ Let two bulls be given to us, and let them choose one bull for themselves and cut it in pieces and lay it on the wood, but put no fire to it. And I will prepare the other bull and lay it on the wood and put no fire to it. ²⁴ And you call upon the name of your god, and I will call upon the name of the Lord, and the God who answers by fire, he is God." And all the people answered, "It is well spoken." ²⁵ Then Elijah said to the prophets of Baal, "Choose for yourselves one bull and prepare it first, for you are many, and call upon the name of your god, but put no fire to it." ²⁶ And they took the bull that was given them, and they prepared it and called upon the name of Baal from morning until noon, saying, "O Baal, answer us!" But there was no voice, and no one answered. And they limped around the altar that they had made. ²⁷ And at noon Elijah mocked them, saying, "Cry aloud, for he is a god. Either he is musing, or he is relieving himself, or he is on a journey, or perhaps he is asleep and must be awakened." ²⁸ And they cried aloud and cut themselves after their custom with swords and lances, until the blood gushed out upon them. ²⁹ And as midday passed, they raved on until the time of the offering of the oblation, but there was no voice. No one answered; no one paid attention.

³⁰ Then Elijah said to all the people, "Come near to me." And all the people came near to him. And he repaired the altar of the Lord that had been thrown down. ³¹ Elijah took twelve stones, according to the number of the tribes of the sons of Jacob, to whom the word of the Lord came, saying, "Israel shall be your name," ³² and with the stones he built an altar in the name of the Lord. And he made a trench about the altar, as great as would contain two seahs of seed. ³³ And he put the wood in order and cut the bull in pieces and laid it on the wood. And he said, "Fill four jars with water and pour it on the burnt offering and on the wood." ³⁴ And he said,

"Do it a second time." And they did it a second time. And he said, "Do it a third time." And they did it a third time. ³⁵ And the water ran around the altar and filled the trench also with water.

³⁶ And at the time of the offering of the oblation, Elijah the prophet came near and said, "O Lord, God of Abraham, Isaac, and Israel, let it be known this day that you are God in Israel, and that I am your servant, and that I have done all these things at your word. ³⁷ Answer me, O Lord, answer me, that this people may know that you, O Lord, are God, and that you have turned their hearts back." ³⁸ Then the fire of the Lord fell and consumed the burnt offering and the wood and the stones and the dust, and licked up the water that was in the trench. ³⁹ And when all the people saw it, they fell on their faces and said, "The Lord, he is God; the Lord, he is God."

John 1:16 ESV

¹⁶ For from his fullness we have all received, grace upon grace.

Ephesians 3:20-21 ESV

²⁰ Now to him who is able to do far more abundantly than all that we ask or think, according to the power at work within us, ²¹ to him be glory in the church and in Christ Jesus throughout all generations, forever and ever. Amen.

Read: 2 Corinthians 12:7-10
Soap: 2 Corinthians 12:8-9

Scripture - Write out the **Scripture** passage for the day.

Observations - Write down 1 or 2 **observations** from the passage.

Applications - Write down 1 or 2 **applications** from the passage.

Pray - Write out a **prayer** over what you learned from today's passage.

Tuesday

Read: 1 Samuel 1:1-20
Soap: 1 Samuel 1:20

Scripture - Write out the **Scripture** passage for the day.

Observations - Write down 1 or 2 **observations** from the passage.

Applications - Write down 1 or 2 **applications** from the passage.

Pray - Write out a **prayer** over what you learned from today's passage.

Read: Psalm 37:7; Lamentations 3:25
Soap: Psalm 37:7

Scripture - Write out the **Scripture** passage for the day.

Observations - Write down 1 or 2 **observations** from the passage.

Wednesday

Applications - Write down 1 or 2 **applications** from the passage.

Pray - Write out a **prayer** over what you learned from today's passage.

-Visit our website today for the corresponding blog post!-

Thursday

Read: 1 Kings 18:20-39
Soap: 1 Kings 18:38-39

Scripture - Write out the **Scripture** passage for the day.

Observations - Write down 1 or 2 **observations** from the passage.

Thursday

Applications - Write down 1 or 2 **applications** from the passage.

Pray - Write out a **prayer** over what you learned from today's passage.

Friday

Read: John 1:16; Ephesians 3:20-21
Soap: John 1:16; Ephesians 3:20

Scripture - Write out the **Scripture** passage for the day.

Observations - Write down 1 or 2 **observations** from the passage.

Applications - Write down 1 or 2 **applications** from the passage.

Pray - Write out a **prayer** over what you learned from today's passage.

Reflection Questions

1. Does God hear everyone's prayers?

2. In what ways have you seen God answer prayer in your life?

3. What should our response be when God says "no"?

4. What encouragement can we give someone who feels that God is being silent?

5. Write down anything new you have learned this week.

My Response

WEEK 7

Week 8

Week 8 Challenge (Note: You can find this listed in our Monday blog post):

Prayer focus for this week: Spend time thanking God for how He is working in your life.

	Praying	Praise
Monday		
Tuesday		
Wednesday		
Thursday		
Friday		

O Lord, in the morning you hear my voice, in the morning I prepare a sacrifice for you and watch.

Psalm 5:3

Psalm 5:3 ESV

³ O Lord, in the morning you hear my voice; in the morning I prepare a sacrifice for you and watch.

Proverbs 8:17 ESV

¹⁷ I love those who love me, and those who seek me diligently find me.

Psalm 63:5-8 ESV

⁵ My soul will be satisfied as with fat and rich food, and my mouth will praise you with joyful lips, ⁶ when I remember you upon my bed, and meditate on you in the watches of the night; ⁷ for you have been my help, and in the shadow of your wings I will sing for joy. ⁸ My soul clings to you; your right hand upholds me.

Psalm 100 ESV

Make a joyful noise to the Lord, all the earth! ² Serve the Lord with gladness! Come into his presence with singing! ³ Know that the Lord, he is God! It is he who made us, and we are his; we are his people, and the sheep of his pasture. ⁴ Enter his gates with thanksgiving, and his courts with praise! Give thanks to him; bless his name! ⁵ For the Lord is good; his steadfast love endures forever, and his faithfulness to all generations.

Psalm 18:1-6 ESV

I love you, O Lord, my strength. ² The Lord is my rock and my fortress and my deliverer, my God, my rock, in whom I take refuge, my shield, and the horn of my salvation, my stronghold. ³ I call upon the Lord, who is worthy to be praised, and I am saved from my enemies.

[4] The cords of death encompassed me; the torrents of destruction assailed me; [5] the cords of Sheol entangled me; the snares of death confronted me.

[6] In my distress I called upon the Lord; to my God I cried for help. From his temple he heard my voice, and my cry to him reached his ears.

Psalm 51 ESV

Have mercy on me, O God, according to your steadfast love; according to your abundant mercy blot out my transgressions. [2] Wash me thoroughly from my iniquity, and cleanse me from my sin!

[3] For I know my transgressions, and my sin is ever before me. [4] Against you, you only, have I sinned and done what is evil in your sight, so that you may be justified in your words and blameless in your judgment. [5] Behold, I was brought forth in iniquity, and in sin did my mother conceive me. [6] Behold, you delight in truth in the inward being, and you teach me wisdom in the secret heart.

[7] Purge me with hyssop, and I shall be clean; wash me, and I shall be whiter than snow. [8] Let me hear joy and gladness; let the bones that you have broken rejoice. [9] Hide your face from my sins, and blot out all my iniquities. [10] Create in me a clean heart, O God, and renew a right spirit within me. [11] Cast me not away from your presence, and take not your Holy Spirit from me. [12] Restore to me the joy of your salvation, and uphold me with a willing spirit.

[13] Then I will teach transgressors your ways, and sinners will return to you. [14] Deliver me from bloodguiltiness, O God, O God of my salvation, and my tongue will sing aloud of your righteousness. [15] O Lord, open my lips, and my mouth will declare your praise. [16] For you will not delight in sacrifice, or I would give it; you will not be pleased with a burnt offering. [17] The sacrifices of God are a broken spirit; a broken and contrite heart, O God, you will not despise.

[18] Do good to Zion in your good pleasure; build up the walls of Jerusalem; [19] then will you delight in right sacrifices, in burnt offerings and whole burnt offerings; then bulls will be offered on your altar.

Monday

Read: Psalm 5:3; Proverbs 8:17
Soap: Psalm 5:3

Scripture - Write out the **Scripture** passage for the day.

Observations - Write down 1 or 2 **observations** from the passage.

Applications - Write down 1 or 2 **applications** from the passage.

Pray - Write out a **prayer** over what you learned from today's passage.

-Visit our website today for the corresponding blog post!-

Read: Psalm 63:5-8
Soap: Psalm 63:5-6

Scripture - Write out the **Scripture** passage for the day.

Observations - Write down 1 or 2 **observations** from the passage.

Tuesday

Applications - Write down 1 or 2 **applications** from the passage.

Pray - Write out a **prayer** over what you learned from today's passage.

Read: Psalm 100
Soap: Psalm 100:4-5

Scripture - Write out the **Scripture** passage for the day.

Observations - Write down 1 or 2 **observations** from the passage.

Wednesday

Applications - Write down 1 or 2 **applications** from the passage.

Pray - Write out a **prayer** over what you learned from today's passage.

Read: Psalm 18:1-6
Soap: Psalm 18:6

Scripture - Write out the **Scripture** passage for the day.

Observations - Write down 1 or 2 **observations** from the passage.

Applications - Write down 1 or 2 **applications** from the passage.

Pray - Write out a **prayer** over what you learned from today's passage.

Read: Psalm 51
Soap: Psalm 51:2-4

Scripture - Write out the **Scripture** passage for the day.

Observations - Write down 1 or 2 **observations** from the passage.

Applications - Write down 1 or 2 **applications** from the passage.

Pray - Write out a **prayer** over what you learned from today's passage.

-Visit our website today for the corresponding blog post!-

Reflection Questions

1. Does it matter when we pray?

2. Read this quote by J.R. Miller:

   "We are often told that we should begin every day with prayer. That is very needful and beautiful. The first face our eyes see in the morning—should be Christ's! His too, should be the first voice we hear; and to Him, our first words should be spoken! Ten minutes in the morning, yes, two minutes, spent really with Christ, will change all our day for us."

   How would our day be different if we spent a few moments with Him in the morning?

3. What gets in the way of you spending time with God in the morning or in the evening? How can you overcome this?

4. Why should you run to God when you sin?

5. What should you do when you don't feel like praying?

My Response

WEEK 8

Made in the USA
San Bernardino, CA
28 April 2017